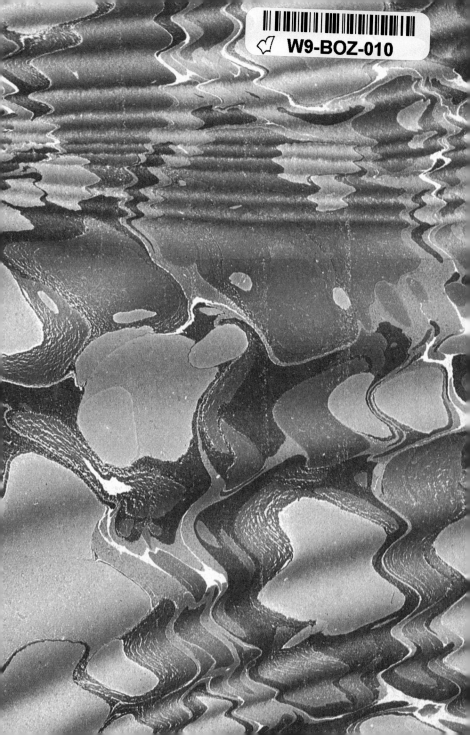

THE VICTORIA AND ALBERT COLOUR BOOKS

LIBRARY OF CONGRESS CATALOGING–IN–PUBLICATION DATA
MAIN ENTRY UNDER TITLE:

THE VICTORIA AND ALBERT COLOUR BOOK OF DECORATIVE ENDPAPERS.

(THE V&A COLOUR BOOKS)
1. ENDPAPERS. 2. BOOK ORNAMENTATION. 3. DECORATIVE
PAPER. I. VICTORIA AND ALBERT MUSEUM. II. TITLE: COLOUR
BOOK OF DECORATIVE ENDPAPERS. III. SERIES.
Z271.V53 1986 686.3'6 85–16551
ISBN 0–8109–1713–0

BOOK, COVER, AND SLIPCASE DESIGN BY COOPER THIRKELL LIMITED

PRODUCTION BY NICK FACER

THE VICTORIA AND ALBERT COLOUR BOOKS

DECORATIVE ENDPAPERS

HARRY N. ABRAMS, INC., PUBLISHERS
NEW YORK

DECORATIVE papers have been used in a variety of ways from the sixteenth century onwards: in book production, as end- and cover-papers, as lining-papers for trunks and deed-boxes, as decoration for cases containing musical instruments[1] and optical instruments, as back patterns for playing cards, and in the nineteenth and twentieth centuries at least, as wrapping papers. Several of the larger scale patterns were also suitable for use as wallpapers, as has been proved by the locations of a few examples. This introduction is intended to give the historical and technical background to the subject and the plates that follow; and to detail the major artists of the genre and some of their creations which the V & A Museum holds. In the main I have not sought to refer to individual papers illustrated because they have been chosen, unapologetically, for their purely *decorative* appeal and not for their importance or influence. If readers wish to see the work of the craftsmen I have mentioned they are welcome to visit the Print Room of the V & A.

Paste Papers. Among the earliest forms of decorated papers are paste papers (German-Kleisterpapier). To make these, a sheet of paper was brushed over with a mixture of flour, water and pigment. Two sheets pressed together, then pulled apart gave a mottled effect. In early specimens the pigments most commonly used were indigo, carmine and burnt sienna. The paste ground which dries rapidly, worked over with tools, such as a

fork or a comb, or with fingers, produces a bold design in white areas or lines. No makers' names are associated with the early paste papers makers, but they were produced in large numbers in Germany in the industry centred on a Moravian community at Herrnhut, Lower Saxony during the second half of the 18th century. Among the most notable exponents of the craft in the present century were Eduard Ludwig of Frankfurt and Ugo Zovetti of Milan.

Chintz Papers. Similar were the 'chintz' papers (German‑Kattunpapier), where the paste ground was printed with woodcut patterns; the blocks, sometimes inlaid with metal pins or strips, were also used to print textiles.

Though thousands of pattern papers were used as book‑covers, a certain number were designed specifically for that purpose, occasionally in imitation of book‑binders' leather tooling.

Dominotier Papers. Another genre of decorative papers are those produced by the 'dominotiers' a name possibly derived from the Italian 'domino', a little cloak or hood which was part of the costume of the men who marbled papers. By the end of the sixteenth century, the dominotiers, centred in Paris, Orleans, Besançon and Tournai were flourishing in France, having joined with some wood engravers in 1586 to form a guild of decorative paper makers, known as 'Dominotiers, Tapissiers, et Imagiers'. Dominotier papers are often characterized by a background powdered with small square dots.

Many pattern papers were also made in Italy, at Bologna, Bassano, Florence and Rome; Antonio Benucci of Florence was among the most productive.

Embossed Papers. Some of the most elegant and luxurious of the decorated

8

papers of the past belong to a group known as 'Dutch gilt' or 'Dutch floral' papers, and in Germany as 'Goldbrokatpapier' (gold brocade papers).

Gold-embossed papers, which were first made at the beginning of the eighteenth century, continued to be produced until about the middle of the nineteenth century. The method of making them was from a deeply-engraved copperplate, heated and covered with imitation gold (or more rarely silver) leaf. The metal used was an alloy of copper, tin, zinc or even lead. The paper which was first coloured by hand or stencilled, was placed on the plate and passed through a roller press. The 'gold' adhered to the lines of the design engraved in the plate, and the surplus was brushed off, leaving the pattern embossed and outlined in gold on the coloured paper. The eighteenth century printers of Augsburg (Boris Ulrich, formenschneider, was the first printer of note), Nuremberg and Fuerth excelled in the manufacture of these papers, as did the Remondini firm, founded in Bassano in 1649, which was still in existence in 1861.

The name 'Dutch gilt' may have originated in the fact that Dutch traders imported the papers into Holland and exported them again to England and France, but Hans Schmoller's suggestion that 'Dutch' may be a corruption of 'Deutsch' (German) seems to be more likely.

The patterns range from naturalistic or fantastic floral and fruit designs to conventional scrolls of acanthus, strapwork and pomegranates, chinoiserie and groups of birds and mythical beasts. Another group contain portraits of saints and worthies, and other figures; these are often divided into separate framed subjects, and are known to the Germans as 'Bilderbogen' (picture sheets); it would seem that they were intended to be cut out. In this category are some blocks of gilded alphabets and numerals.

Georg Christoph Stoy (1670-1750), was born in Nuremberg, became a paper-embosser in Augsburg, where he married the

9

widow of the painter and papermaker Mathias Fröhlich, whose business he took over, which included from 1790, his imperial 'Privilegium impressorum' for leather and metallic papers. Some of Stoy's patterns are related to woven silk designs. Johann Michael Schwibecher (1695-1748), with whom Stoy had a disagreement in 1739, worked in Augsburg from 1715 (in which year he married the widow of J. M. Munck the Elder), until his death. His plate from which a pattern paper[2] was printed, showing a huntsman, and figures in Persian costume amid scrolling acanthus stems, was bought from his effects by Marx Leonard Kauffmann (worked x. 1761-c.1772), who printed it with his own address *Augsburg Bey Marx Leonard Kaufman N 34*.

Johann Michael Reimund (c.1727-1768), the first of the Nuremberg paper-embossers, made a copy in reverse of Schwibecher's design. A paper with a design of large birds eating berries was issued by Andreas Reimund (worked c.1755-died 1782), and re-issued with the address of J. M. Reimund, *M R*.

Paul Reimund (1764-1815), the son of Andreas, lived in the Weissgerbergasse, Nuremberg, where he employed six workmen, c.1800. In 1803 he is listed as a master in the Nuremberg Formschneiderbuch (pattern-makers book); his widow was still in business in 1820. George Daniel Reimund, who also died in 1815 was his younger brother (born 1770). A pattern of small stems and pods is signed *Georg Daniel*, but is identical with another impression bearing Paul's address, numbered *30*[3].

A fine chinoiserie paper was produced by Johann Köchel (1682-1726), of Fuerth; the design shows figures in eastern costume, beneath date palms, and seated at tables, drinking and smoking, with pagodas, between acanthus leaves and strapwork. Köchel may have derived his chinoiserie figures from the scenes engraved after Elias Baeck (1669-1747) (called

Heldenmuth) of Augsburg, or from the rococo chinoiserie of Johann Esaias Nilson (1721-1788). Other makers of chinoiserie patterns include Georg Popp (c.1710-1735) of Fuerth and Johann Friedrich Leopold (1669-1727), of Augsburg. In 1726 the latter obtained the 'Privilegium impressorum'.

Johann Carl Munck (c.1730-1794), son of J. M. Munck the Younger (c.1710-1762), made embossed papers at Augsburg from about 1749; a paper with a design emblematic of the Seasons shows the figures of Winter and Spring, with skaters, and men sowing and ploughing, in the backgrounds, within rich rococo ornament. This rococo framework which surrounds the figures, is according to Haemmerle, a rare example of the use of rococo motifs in brocade papers; he cites only one other 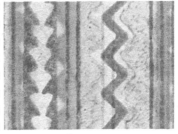 design, also by J. M. Munck, a 'Bilderbogen', in which the figures of saints are within rococo framework. The rustic figures engraved after Gottfried Bernhard Göetz (Göz) (1708-1774) or Johann Bergmüller (1688-1762), of Augsburg, are likely to have provided Munck with some of the elements in his design. The paper, moreover has been designed in the form of a book-cover. Other genre scenes produced by the decorative paper makers probably owed some of their motifs to the various 'Trachtenbücher' (costume books) of the period, in particular, Munck's 'Bilderbogen' with scenes of artists and artisans at work, which was copied in reverse by Paul Reimund.

Two papers in the V & A's collection, one by Johann Georg Eder (worked c.1762-c.1800), of Augsburg, who married J. M. Munck's widow in 1762, the other by J. W. Meyer, are embossed papers which have been successfully 'patroniert' (stamped with wood blocks, or stencilled) in pleasing colours.

The production of the 'Bilderbogen' continued well into the nineteenth

century, as is illustrated by a
gold-embossed scene depicting the
departure of the train from
Nuremberg on 'Ludwig's Eisen'
bahn', the first German railway line,
connecting Nuremberg to Fuerth,
which was opened on 7 December
1835.

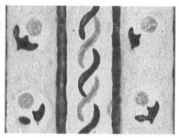

In 1796 a patent was granted to John Gregory Hancock for 'paper ornamented by embossing and chasing', but the only surviving example of an English paper in this genre is by Benjamin Moore of 31 Newgate Street, London, and is dated *1763*[4]. Moore received a premium from the Society of Arts in 1764 for the introduction of the manufacture of embossed papers to this country; he was possibly connected with the firm of Moore & Gough, paperhangers in Aldgate from 1774 until 1840 (then entered in the directory as Moore & Co.).

Marbled Papers. The marbling of paper was practised in the Near East centuries before it became known in Europe. Basically the art consists of floating colours, mixed with ox or fish gall, on a decoction of carrageen moss, or in earlier times, a mixture of Fleawort seed and gum tragacanth, and mingling them in a variety of ways by combing, using a stick, or simply by agitating the surface of the liquid until a wave pattern is formed. A sheet of moistened paper is then floated on the surface and the patterned colours adhere to it. Turkish marbled papers are classified in twelve types; that known as 'Hatip-Ebrusu' (preacher marble) was invented by a preacher in the Hagia Sophia in the eighteenth century, and is florally decorated.

The invention of marbling in Europe is ascribed by Jean La Caille[5] to Mace Ruette, a Parisian stationer and bookbinder, working about 1606, but a similar claim is made for a German origin. As with the invention of flocked paper, the question of country of origin is unresolved, but according to Zaehnsdorf[6] marbled papers were first imported into England about the middle of the seventeenth century as wrappers for toys from Nuremberg, and the wrappers were sold to the bookbinders, who used them as end- and lining-papers. Joseph W Zaehnsdorf, himself an eminent nineteenth century bookbinder, was also the maker of beautiful and original marbled papers.

A type of marbling made by chemical reaction, rather than by combing or other 'mechanical' means, was known to the Turks and was obtained by using spirit of soap, which formed disintegration patterns in the colours. A re-discovery of this method in the eighteenth century is shown in the so-called 'Stormont' marbling, with the 'laced' blue colour, made by adding turpentine. The earliest identification of Stormont marbling is in a *Book of Common Prayer*, printed in Dublin in 1750. A nineteenth century German chemical pattern is known as 'Sonnenmarmor' (sun marble).

Two outstanding makers of marbled papers in England in this century were Tirzah Garwood (Mrs Eric Ravilious) (1908-1951), who used a chemical reaction method, and Douglas Cockerell, whose highly skilled and distinguished work is within the traditional methods of combed marbled papers.

A far wider range than is here described, of decorative papers of all periods is contained in the Museum's collection, and includes the batik and lithographic papers, produced by the Münchener Tapetfabrik in the 1920's and 1930's, also the book papers made by the Curwen Press during the same era, designed by such artists as Paul Nash, Enid Marx, Edward Bawden and Claude Lovat Fraser. The craft of the decorative papermaker through the centuries has provided us with a microcosm of the uses of ornament in less ephemeral media, and has added to the scope of decorative design by the art of marbling, and the unique forms of the paste pattern.

[1] An example is a boder, printed by G. C. Stoy of Augsburg, which adorns a harpsichord.

[2] An impression was attached to a calendar for 1738 (V & A Library, No. L.1321-1888).

[3] Not the same pattern as the one unrecorded in Haemmerle, issued by Paul Reimund with the same number

[4] Another impression is in the R. B. Loring Collection, Cambridge, USA.

[5] La Caille, *Histoire de l'imprimerie*, Paris, 1689.

[6] J. W. Zaehnsdorf, *The Art of Bookbinding*, London, 1880.

BIBLIOGRAPHY

Adolf Halbey, 'Lob des Buntpapiers', *Insel-Almanach*, 1963.

Albert Haemmerle, *Buntpapier*, Munich, 1961, 2nd ed. 1977.

Dr. E. W. Mick, *Altes Buntpapier*, Dortmund, 1979.

Mirjam M Foot, 'The Olga Hirsch Collection of Decorated Papiers', *The British Library Journal*, Vol.7, pt.1, 1981.

Hans Schmoller, *Panoply of Paper: on Collecting Decorated Papers*, Reprint from *Matrix 3*, The Whittington Press, Andoversford, 1983.

A. Haemmerle, 'Augsburger Buntpapier', *Viertel Jahres hefte zur Kunst und Geschichte Augsburgs*, Jahrgang III, October-March, 1937-38.

Mehmed Ali Kagitoi, 'Turkish Marbled Papers', *Palette*, No.30, 1968.

THE PLATES

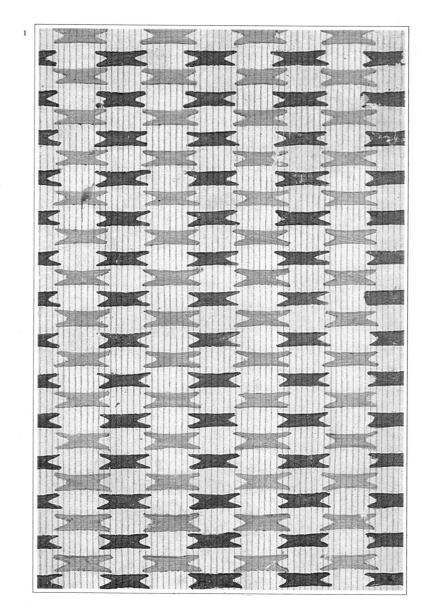

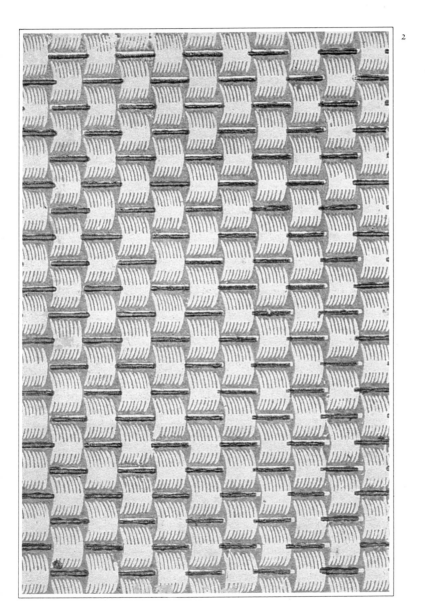

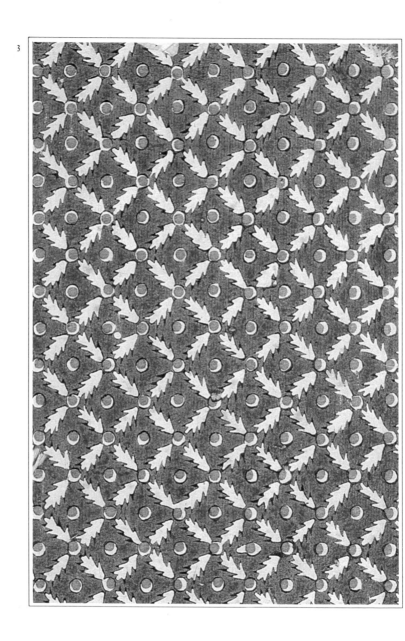

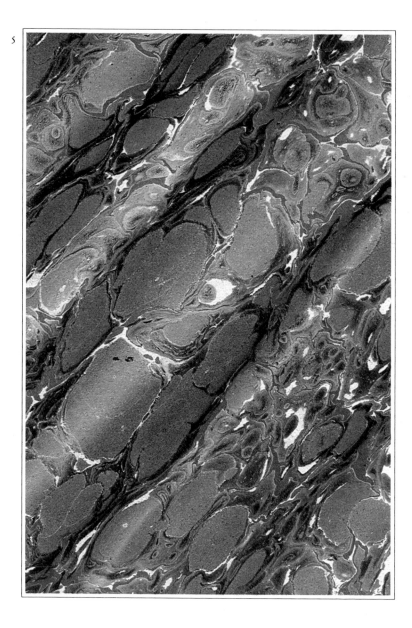

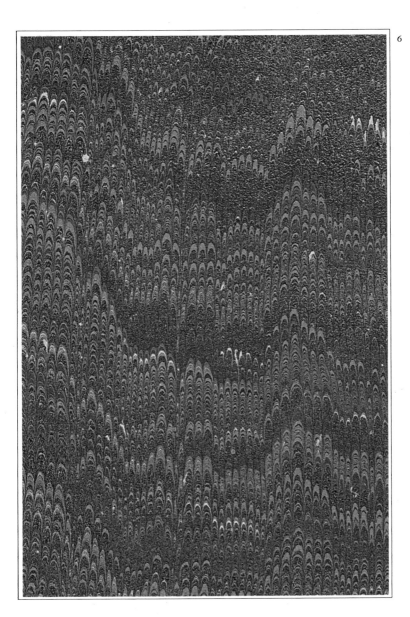

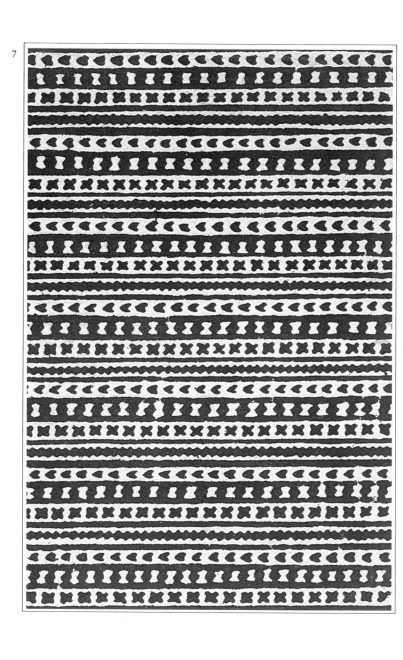

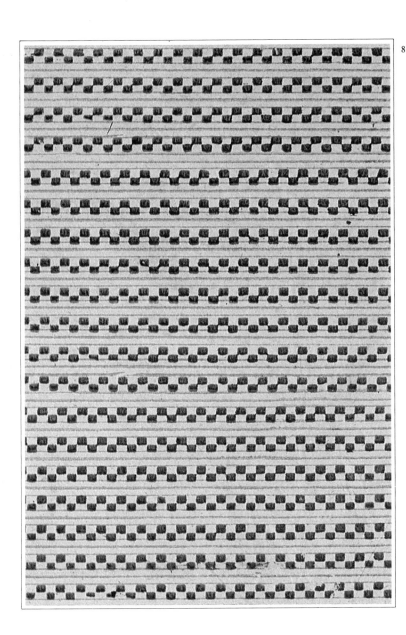

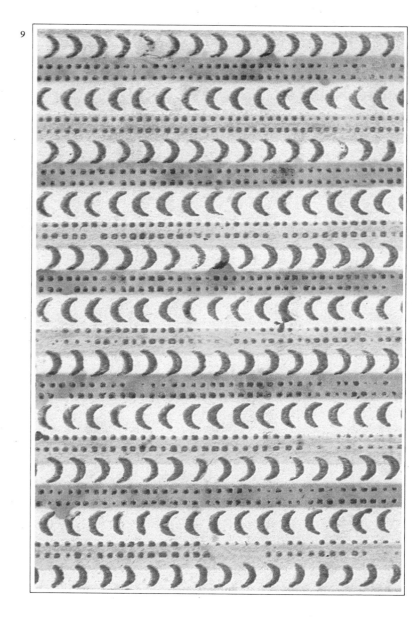

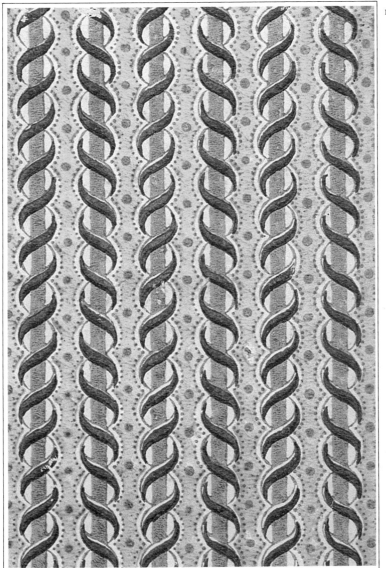

11

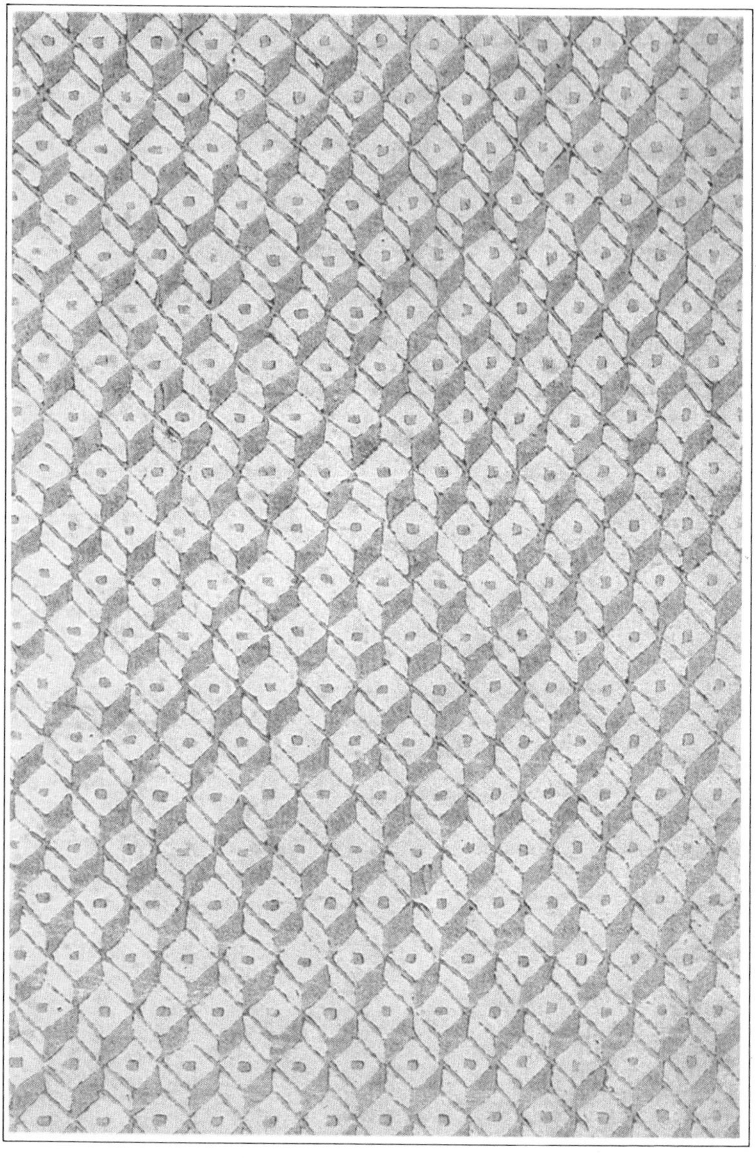

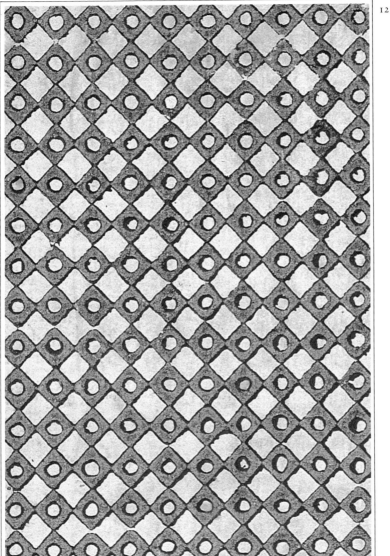

13

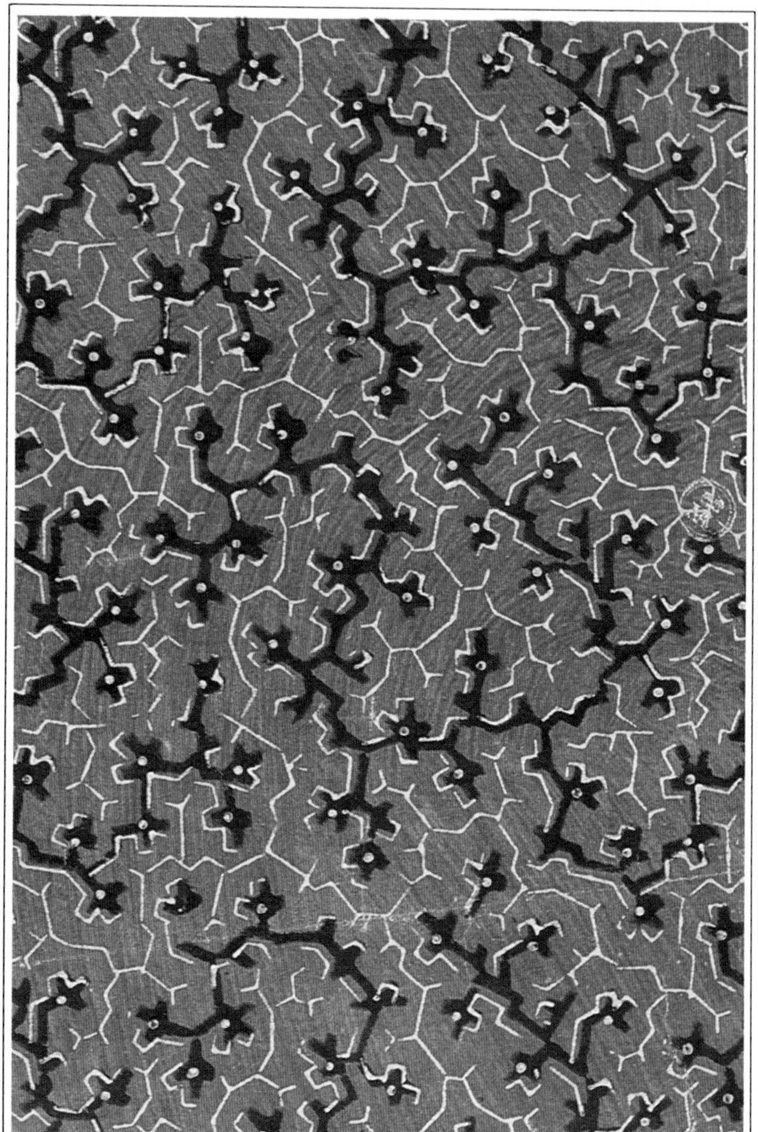

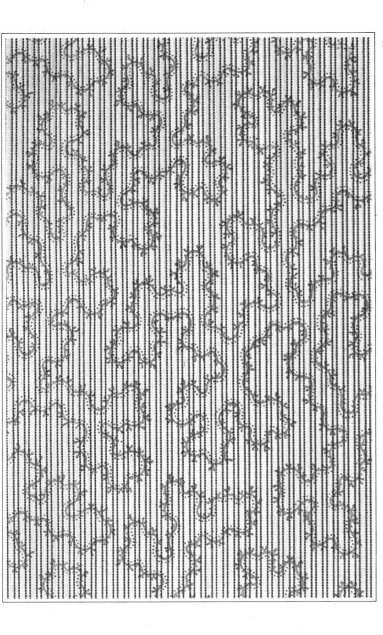

15

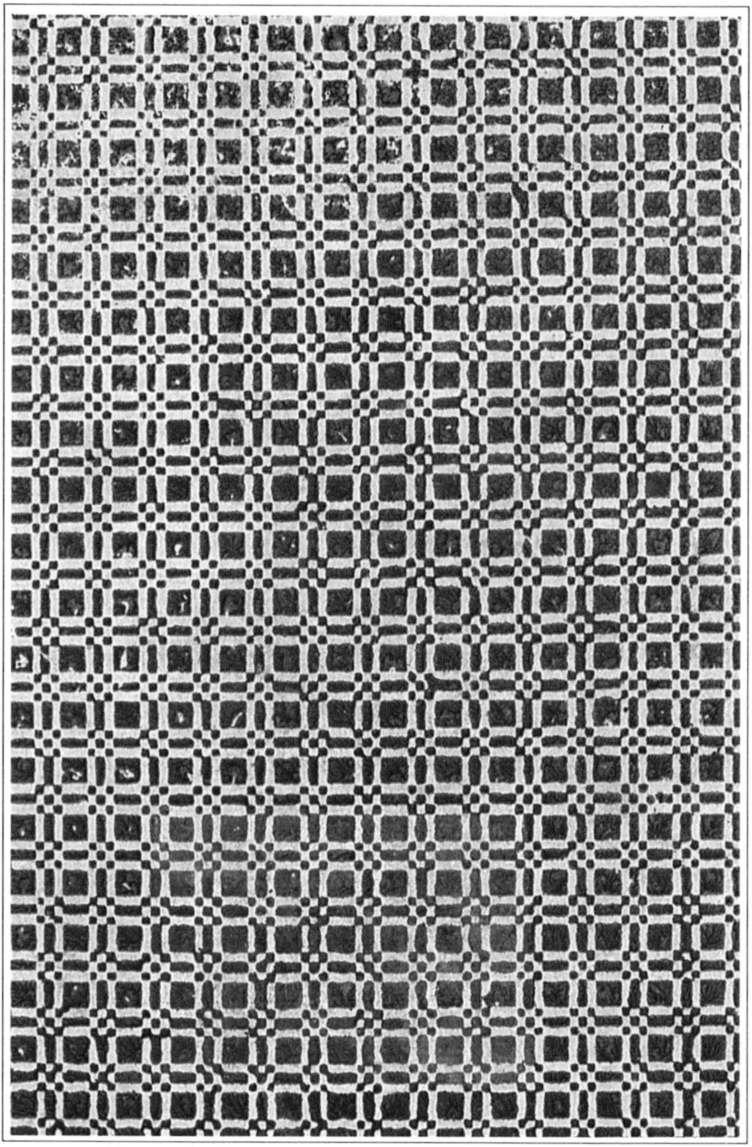

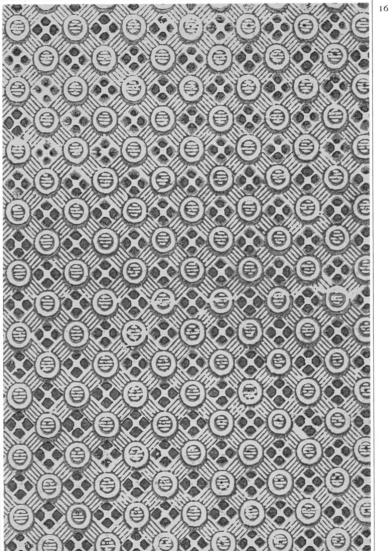

17

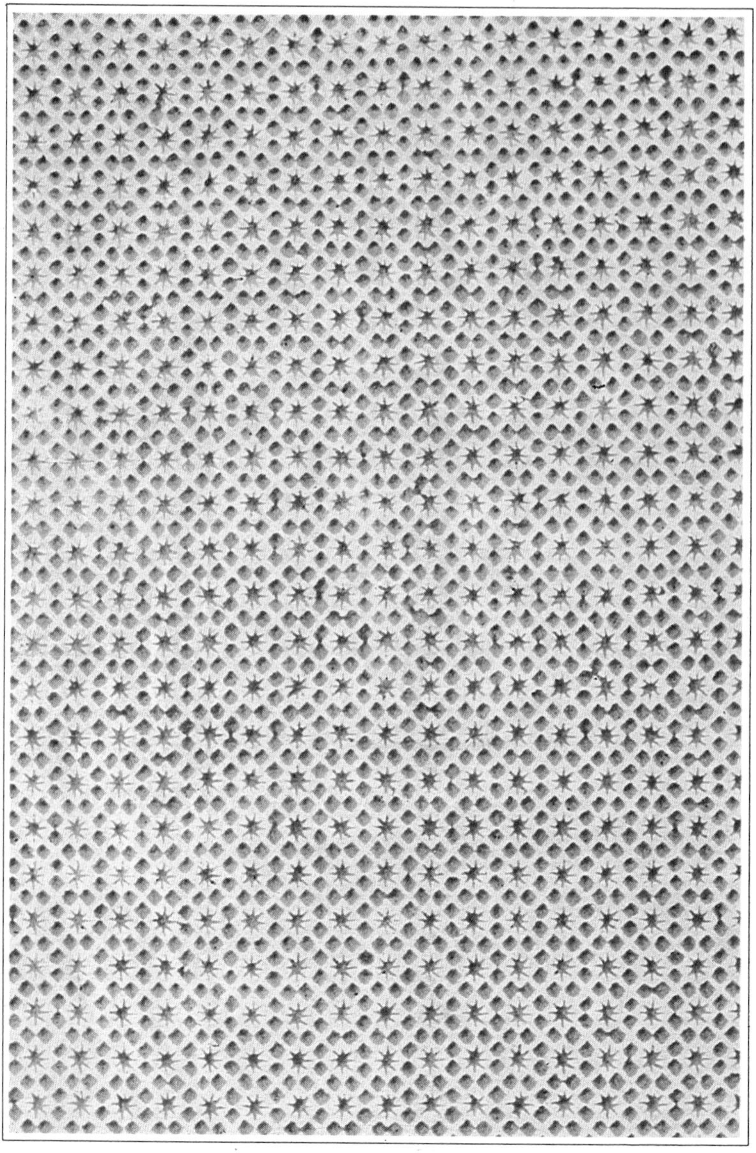

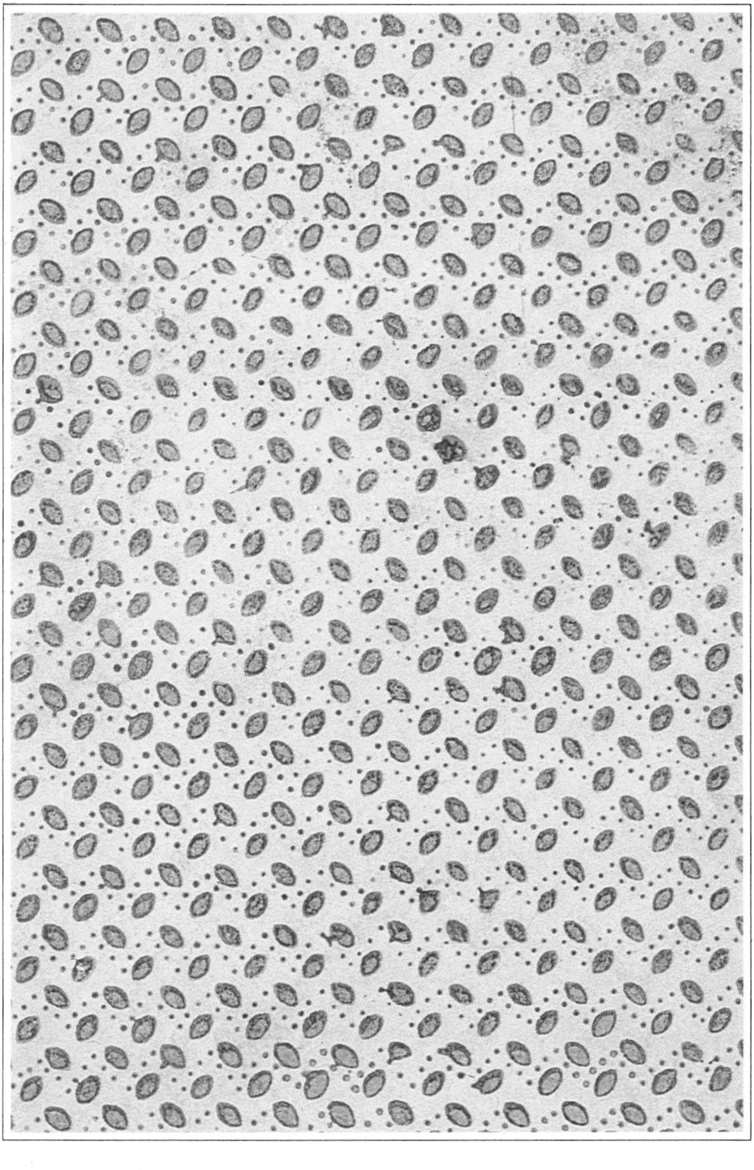

18

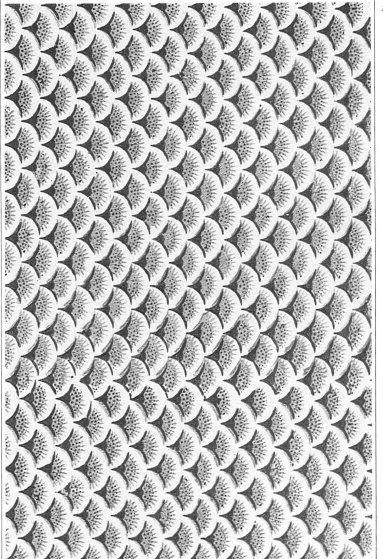

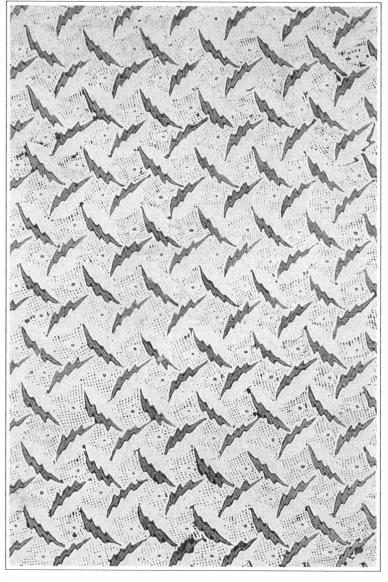

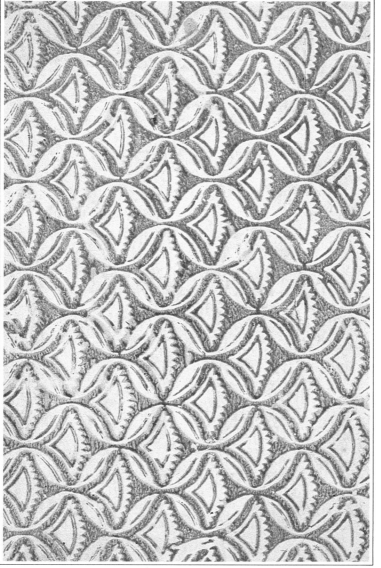

27

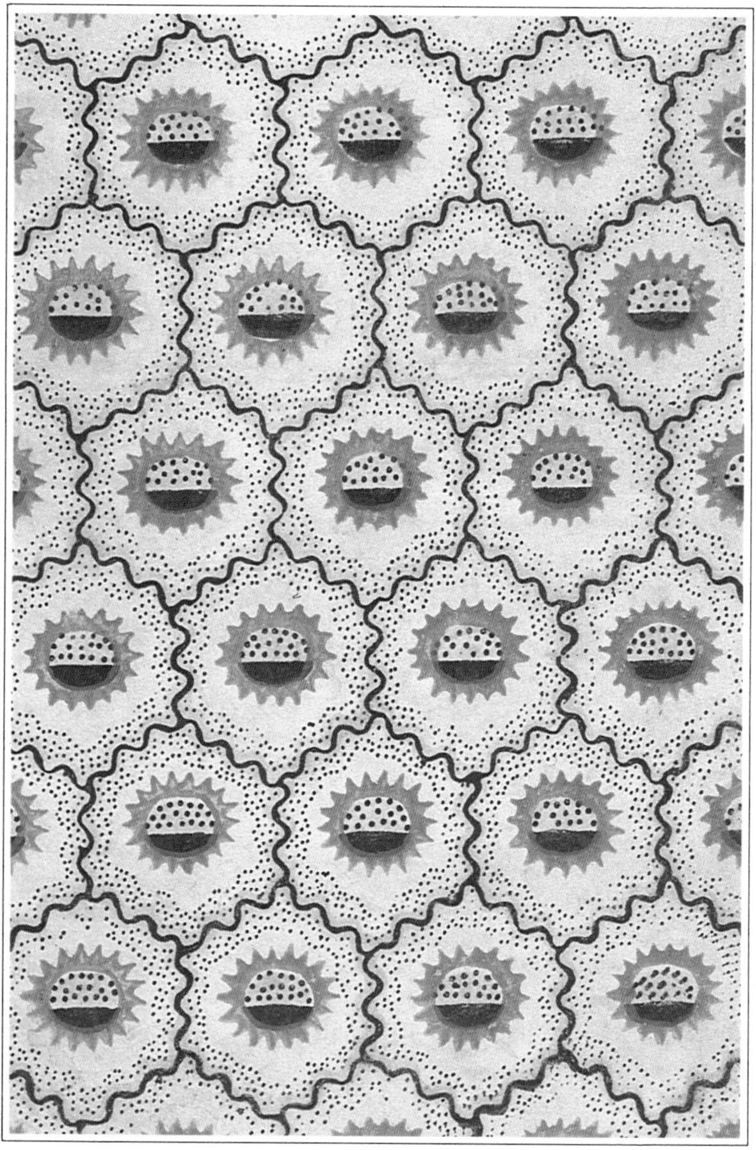

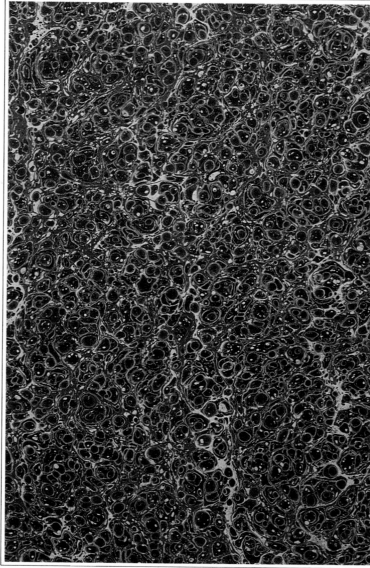

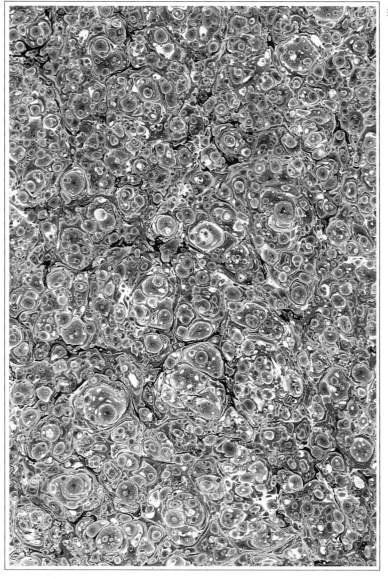

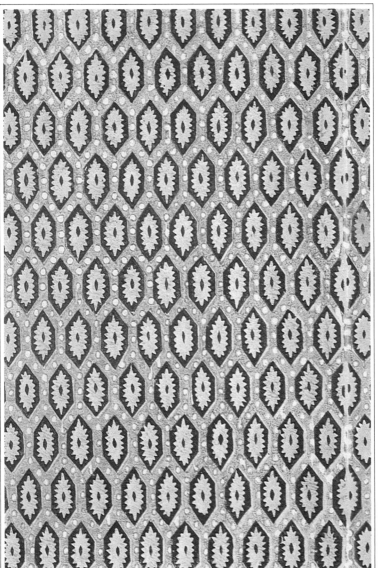

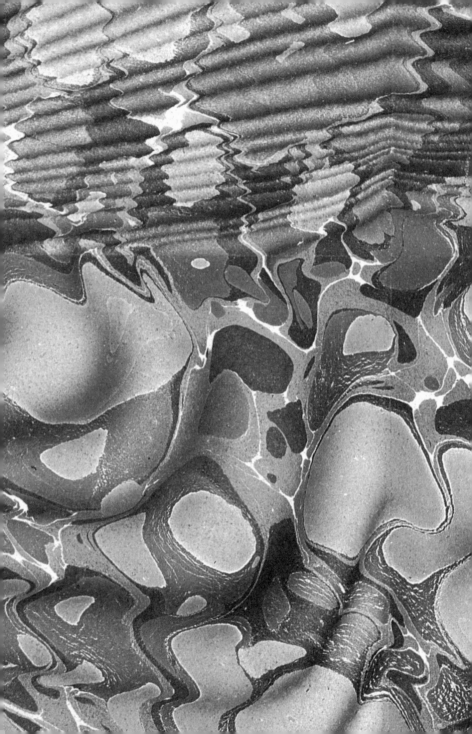